On Receiving the First
Aspen Award

On Receiving the First Aspen Award

A Speech by
BENJAMIN BRITTEN

FABER MUSIC
in association with
FABER AND FABER
London

First published in 1964
by Faber and Faber Limited
Second impression 1978
by Faber Music Limited
3 Queen Square London WC1N 3AU
Printed in Great Britain
by Halstan & Co Ltd

Britten, Benjamin, *Baron Britten*
   On receiving the first Aspen Award.
   1. Music
   I. Title
   780   ML160

   ISBN 0-571-10023-6

ISBN 0 571 10023 6

Publishers' Note

Benjamin Britten was altogether happier writing notes rather than words. However, in his Aspen Award Speech of 1964 he set down at some length some of the beliefs and ideals that were clearly important to him as an artist. It remains the only statement of its kind that Britten made, and we are grateful to the Executors of the Britten Estate for permission to reprint the speech, which has long been out of print and for the re-issue of which there has been widespread demand.

D.M.
1977

The Aspen Award and Aspen Institute for Humanistic Studies

The Robert O. Anderson Aspen Award in the Humanities was established in 1963 to honour 'the individual anywhere in the world judged to have made the greatest contribution to the advancement of the humanities'.

Benjamin Britten was chosen as the first recipient of the Award from among more than a hundred artists, scholars, writers, poets, philosophers, and statesmen, who had been nominated by leaders in intellectual and cultural fields throughout the world.

The Award was presented by Alvin C. Eurich, President of the Aspen Institute, at a ceremony in the Aspen Amphitheatre, Aspen, Colorado, on 31st July, 1964. The Citation read:

'To Benjamin Britten,
who, as a brilliant composer, performer, and interpreter through music of human feelings, moods, and thoughts, has truly inspired man to understand, clarify and appreciate more fully his own nature, purpose and destiny.'

On Receiving the First Aspen Award

Ladies and Gentlemen, when last May your Chairman and your President told me they wished to travel the 5000 miles from Aspen to Aldeburgh to have a talk with me, they hinted that it had something to do with an Aspen Award for Services to the Humanities—an award of very considerable importance and size. I imagined that they felt I might advise them on a suitable recipient, and I began to consider what I should say. Who would be suitable for such an honour? What kind of person? Doctor? Priest? A social worker? A politician? Well, . . .! An artist? Yes, possibly (that, I imagined, could be the reason that Mr. Anderson and Professor Eurich thought I might be the person to help them). So I ran through the names of the great figures working in the Arts among us today. It was a fascinating problem; rather like one's school-time game of ideal cricket elevens, or slightly more recently, ideal casts for operas—but I certainly won't tell which of our great poets, painters, or composers came to the top of my list.

Mr. Anderson and Professor Eurich paid their visit to my home in Aldeburgh. It was a charming and courteous visit, but it was also a knock-out. It had not occurred to me, frankly, that it was I who was to be the recipient of this magnificent award, and I was stunned. I am afraid my friends must have felt I was a tongue-tied host. But I simply could not imagine why *I* had been chosen for this very great honour. I read again the simple and moving citation. The key-word seemed to be 'humanities'. I went to the dictionary to look up its meaning, I found *Humanity*: 'the quality of being human' (well, that applied to me all right). But I found that the plural had a special meaning: 'Learning or literature concerned with human culture, as grammar, rhetoric, poetry and especially the ancient Latin and Greek Classics'. (Here I really had no claims since I cannot properly spell even in my own language, and when I set Latin I have terrible trouble over the quantities—besides you can all hear how far removed I am from rhetoric.) *Humanitarian* was an entry close beside these, and I supposed I might have some claim here, but I was daunted by the definition: 'One who goes to excess in his human principles (in 1855 often contemptuous or hostile)'. I read on, quickly. *Humanist*: 'One versed in Humanities', and I was back where I started. But perhaps after all the clue was in the word 'human', and I began to feel that I might have a small claim.

II

I certainly write music for human beings—directly and deliberately. I consider their voices, the range, the power, the subtlety, and the colour potentialities of them. I consider the instruments they play—their most expressive and suitable individual sonorities, and where I may be said to have invented an instrument (such as the Slung Mugs of *Noye's Fludde*) I have borne in mind the pleasure the young performers will have in playing it. I also take note of the *human* circumstances of music, of its environment and conventions; for instance, I try to write dramatically effective music for the theatre—I certainly don't think opera is better for not being effective on the stage (some people think that effectiveness *must* be superficial). And then the best music to listen to in a great Gothic church is the polyphony which was written for it, and was calculated for its resonance: this was my approach in the *War Requiem*—I calculated it for a big, reverberant acoustic and that is where it sounds best. I believe, you see, in *occasional music*, although I admit there are some occasions which can intimidate one—I do not envy Purcell writing his *Ode to Celebrate King James's Return to London from Newmarket*. On the other hand almost every piece I have ever written has been composed with a certain occasion in mind, and usually for definite performers, and certainly always *human* ones.

III

You may ask perhaps: how far can a composer go in thus considering the demands of people, of humanity? At many times in history the artist has made a conscious effort to speak with the voice of the people. Beethoven certainly tried, in works as different as the *Battle of Vittoria* and the Ninth Symphony, to utter the sentiments of a whole community. From the beginning

of Christianity there have been musicians who have
wanted and tried to be the servants of the church, and
to express the devotion and convictions of Christians,
as such. Recently, we have had the example of Shosta-
kovich, who set out in his 'Leningrad' Symphony to
present a monument to his fellow citizens, an explicit
expression for them of their own endurance and hero-
ism. At a very different level, one finds composers such
as Johann Strauss and George Gershwin aiming at pro-
viding people—the people—with the best dance music
and songs which they were capable of making. And I
can find nothing wrong with the objectives—declared
or implicit—of these men; nothing wrong with offering
to my fellow-men music which may inspire them or
comfort them, which may touch them or entertain
them, even educate them—directly and with intention.
On the contrary, it is the composer's duty, as a member
of society, to speak to or for his fellow human beings.

When I am asked to compose a work for an occasion, great or small, I want to know in some detail
the conditions of the place where it will be performed,
the size and acoustics, what instruments or singers
will be available and suitable, the kind of people who
will hear it, and what language they will understand—
and even sometimes the age of the listeners and performers. For it is futile to offer children music by
which they are bored, or which makes them feel in-
adequate or frustrated, which may set them against
music forever; and it is insulting to address anyone in
a language which they do not understand. The text of

my *War Requiem* was perfectly in place in Coventry Cathedral—the Owen poems in the vernacular, and the words of the Requiem Mass familiar to everyone—but it would have been pointless in Cairo or Peking.

During the act of composition one is continually referring back to the conditions of performance—as I have said, the acoustics and the forces available, the techniques of the instruments and the voices—such questions occupy one's attention continuously, and certainly affect the stuff of the music, and in my experience are not only a restriction, but a challenge, an inspiration. Music does not exist in a vacuum, it does not exist until it is performed, and performance imposes conditions. It is the easiest thing in the world to write a piece virtually or totally impossible to perform —but oddly enough that is not what I prefer to do; I prefer to study the conditions of performance and shape my music to them.

IV

Where does one stop, then, in answering people's demands? It seems that there is no clearly defined Halt sign on this road. The only brake which one can apply is that of one's own private and personal conscience; when that speaks clearly, one must halt; and it can speak for musical or non-musical reasons. In the last six months I have been several times asked to write a work as a memorial to the late President Kennedy. On each occasion I have refused—not because in any way I was out of sympathy with such an idea; on the contrary, I was horrified and deeply moved by the tragic death of a very remarkable man. But for me I do not feel the time is ripe; I cannot yet stand back and see it clear. I should have to wait very much longer to do anything like justice to this great theme. But had I in fact agreed to undertake a limited commission, my artistic conscience would certainly have told me in what direction I could go, and when I should have to stop.

There are many dangers which hedge round the unfortunate composer: pressure groups which demand true proletarian music, snobs who demand the latest *avant-garde* tricks; critics who are already trying to document today for tomorrow, to be the first to find the correct pigeon-hole definition. These people are dangerous—not because they are necessarily of any importance in themselves, but because they may make the composer, above all the young composer, self-conscious, and instead of writing his own music, music which springs naturally from his gift and personality, he may be frightened into writing pretentious nonsense or deliberate obscurity. He may find himself writing more and more for machines, in conditions dictated by machines, and not by humanity: or of course he may end by creating grandiose clap-trap when his real talent is for dance tunes or children's piano pieces. Finding one's place in society as a composer is not a straightforward job. It is not helped by the attitude towards the composer in some societies. My own, for instance, semi-Socialist Britain, and Conservative Britain before it, has for years treated the musician as a curiosity to be barely tolerated. At a tennis party in my youth I was asked what I was going to do when I grew up—what job I was aiming at. 'I am going to be a composer', I said. 'Yes, but what else?' was the answer. The average Briton thought, and still thinks, of the Arts as suspect and expensive luxuries. The Manchester councillor who boasted he had never been to a concert and didn't intend to go, is no very rare bird in England. By Act of Parliament, each local authority in England is empowered to spend a sixpenny rate on the Arts. In fact it seems that few of them spend more than one twentieth of this—a sign of no very great enthusiasm! Until such a condition is changed, musicians will continue to feel 'out of step' in our semi-Welfare State.

But if we in England have to face a considerable indifference, in other countries conditions can have other, equally awkward effects. In totalitarian regimes, we know that great official pressure is used to bring the artist into line and make him conform to the State's ideology. In the richer capitalist countries, money and snobbishness combine to demand the latest, newest manifestations, which I am told go by the name in this country of 'Foundation Music'.

v

The *ideal* conditions for an artist or musician will never be found outside the *ideal* society, and when shall we see that? But I think I can tell you some of the things which any artist demands from any society. He demands that his art shall be accepted as an essential part of human activity, and human expression; and that he shall be accepted as a genuine practitioner of that art and consequently of value to the community; reasonably, he demands from society a secure living and a pension when he has worked long enough; this is a basis for society to offer a musician, a modest basis. In actual fact there are very few musicians in my country who will get a pension after forty years' work in an orchestra or in an opera house. This must be changed; we must at least be treated as civil servants. Once we have a material status, we can accept the responsibility of answering society's demands on us. And society should and will demand from us the utmost of our skill and gift in the full range of music-making. (Here we come back to 'occasional' music.) There should be special music made and played for all sorts of occasions: football matches, receptions, elections (why not?) and even presentations of awards! I would have been delighted to have been greeted with a special piece composed for today! It might have turned out to be another piece as good as the cantata Bach wrote for the Municipal Election at Mühlhausen, or the Galliard that Dowland wrote as a compliment to the Earl of Essex! Some of the greatest pieces of music in our possession were written for special occasions, grave or gay. But we shouldn't worry too much about the so-called 'permanent' value of our occasional music. A lot of it cannot make much sense after its first performance, and it is quite a good thing to please people, even if only for today. That is what we should aim at—pleasing people today as seriously as we can, and letting the future look after itself. Bach wrote his *St. Matthew Passion* for performance on one day of the year only—the day which in the Christian church was the culmination of the year, to which the year's worship was leading. It is one of the unhappiest results of the march of science and commerce that this unique work, at the turn of a switch, is at the mercy of any loud roomful of cocktail drinkers—to be listened to or switched off at will, without ceremony or occasion.

VI

The wording of your Institute's Constitution implies an effort to present the Arts as a counter-balance to Science in today's life. And though I am sure you do not imagine that there is not a lot of science, knowledge and skill in the art of making music (in the calculation of sound qualities and colours, the knowledge of the technique of instruments and voices, the balance of forms, the creation of moods, and in the development of ideas), I would like to think you are suggesting that what is important in the Arts is *not* the scientific part, the analysable part of music, but the something which emerges from it but transcends it, which cannot be analysed because it is not *in* it, but *of* it. It is the quality which cannot be acquired by simply the exercise of a technique or a system: it is something to do with personality, with gift, with

17

spirit. I quite simply call it—magic: a quality which would appear to be by no means unacknowledged by scientists, and which I value more than any other part of music.

It is arguable that the richest and most productive eighteen months in our music history is the time when Beethoven had just died, when the other nineteenth-century giants, Wagner, Verdi and Brahms had not begun; I mean the period in which Franz Schubert wrote his *Winterreise*, the C major Symphony, his last three piano sonatas, the C major String Quintet, as well as a dozen other glorious pieces. The very creation of these works in that space of time seems hardly credible; but the standard of inspiration, of magic, is miraculous and past all explanation. Though I have worked very hard at the *Winterreise* the last five years, every time I come back to it I am amazed not only by the extraordinary mastery of it—for Schubert knew exactly what he was doing (make no mistake about that), and he had thought profoundly about it—but by the renewal of the magic: each time, the mystery remains.

This magic comes only with the sounding of the music, with the turning of the written note into sound —and it only comes (or comes most intensely) when the listener is one with the composer, either as a performer himself, or as a listener in active sympathy. Simply to read a score in one's armchair is not enough for evoking this quality. Indeed, this magic can be said to consist of just the music which is *not* in the score.

Sometimes one can be quite daunted when one opens the *Winterreise*—there seems to be nothing on the page. One must not exaggerate—the shape of the music in Schubert is clearly visible. What *cannot* be indicated on the printed page are the innumerable small variants of rhythm and phrasing which make up the performer's contribution. In the *Winterreise*, it was not possible for Schubert to indicate exactly the length of rests and pauses, or the colour of the singer's voice or the clarity or smoothness of consonants. This is the responsibility of each individual performer, and at each performance he will make modifications. The composer expects him to; he would be foolish if he did not. For a musical experience needs three human beings at least. It requires a composer, a performer, and a listener; and unless these three take part together there is no musical experience. The experience will be that much more intense and rewarding if the circumstances correspond to what the composer intended: if the *St. Matthew Passion* is performed on Good Friday in a church, to a congregation of Christians; if the *Winterreise* is performed in a room, or in a small hall of truly intimate character to a circle of friends; if *Don Giovanni* is played to an audience which understands the text and appreciates the musical allusions. The further one departs from these circumstances, the less true and more diluted is the experience likely to be.

One must face the fact today that the vast majority of musical performances take place as far away from the original as it is possible to imagine: I do not mean simply *Falstaff* being given in Tokyo, or the Mozart Requiem in Madras. I mean of course that such works *can* be audible in any corner of the globe, at any moment of the day or night, through a loudspeaker, without question of suitability or comprehensibility. Anyone, anywhere, at any time, can listen to the B minor Mass upon one condition only—that they possess a machine. No qualification is required of any sort—faith, virtue, education, experience, age. Music is now free for all. If I say the loudspeaker is the principal enemy of music, I don't mean that I am not grateful to it as a means of education or study, or as an evoker of memories. But it is not part of true musical *experience*. Regarded as such it is simply a substitute, and dangerous because deluding. Music demands more from a listener than simply the possession of a tape-machine or a transistor radio. It demands some preparation, some effort, a journey to a special place, saving up for a ticket, some homework on the programme perhaps, some clarification of the ears and sharpening of the instincts. It demands as much effort on the listener's part as the other two corners of the triangle, this holy triangle of composer, performer and listener.

VII

Ladies and Gentlemen, this award is the latest of the kindnesses for which I am indebted to your country. I first came to the United States twenty-five years ago,

at the time when I was a discouraged young composer
—muddled, fed-up and looking for work, longing to
be used. I was most generously treated here, by old
and new friends, and to all of these I can never be
sufficiently grateful. Their kindness was past descrip-
tion; I shall never forget it. But the thing I am *most*
grateful to your country for is this: it was in California,
in the unhappy summer of 1941, that, coming across a
copy of the Poetical Works of George Crabbe in a
Los Angeles bookshop, I first read his poem, *Peter
Grimes*; and, at this same time, reading a most percep-
tive and revealing article about it by E. M. Forster,
I suddenly realised where I belonged and what I
lacked. I had become without roots, and when I got
back to England six months later I was ready to put
them down. I have lived since then in the same small
corner of East Anglia, near where I was born. And I
find as I get older that working becomes more and
more difficult away from that home. Of course, I plot
and plan my music when I am away on tour, and I get
great stimulus and excitement from visiting other
countries; with a congenial partner I like giving con-
certs, and in the last years we have travelled as far as
Vancouver and Tokyo, Moscow and Java; I like
making new friends, meeting new audiences, hearing
new music. But I belong at home—there—in Aldeburgh. I have tried to bring music *to* it in the shape of
our local Festival; and all the music I write comes *from*
it. I believe in roots, in associations, in backgrounds,
in personal relationships. I want my music to be of

use to people, to please them, to 'enhance their lives' (to use Berenson's phrase). I do not write for posterity —in any case, the outlook for that is somewhat uncertain. I write music, now, in Aldeburgh, for people living there, and further afield, indeed for anyone who cares to play it or listen to it. But my music now has its roots, in where I live and work. And I only came to realise that in California in 1941.

VIII

People have already asked me what I am going to do with your money; I have even been told in the post and in the press exactly how I ought to dispose of it. I shall of course pay no attention to these suggestions, however well- or ill-intentioned. The last prize I was given went straight away to the Aldeburgh Festival, the musical project I have most at heart. It would not surprise me if a considerable part of the Aspen Award went in that direction; I have not really decided. But one thing I know I want to do; I should like to give an annual Aspen Prize for a British composition. The conditions would change each year; one year it might be for a work for young voices and a school orchestra, another year for the celebration of a national event or centenary, another time a work for an instrument whose repertory is small; but in any case for specific or general usefulness. And the Jury would be instructed to choose only that work which was a pleasure to perform and inspiriting to listen to. In this way I would try to express my interpretation of the intention behind the Aspen Institute, and to express my warmest thanks, my most humble thanks, for the honour which you have awarded me today.